This coloring book belongs to:

_____

Petey the Pumpkin (and his patch pals)

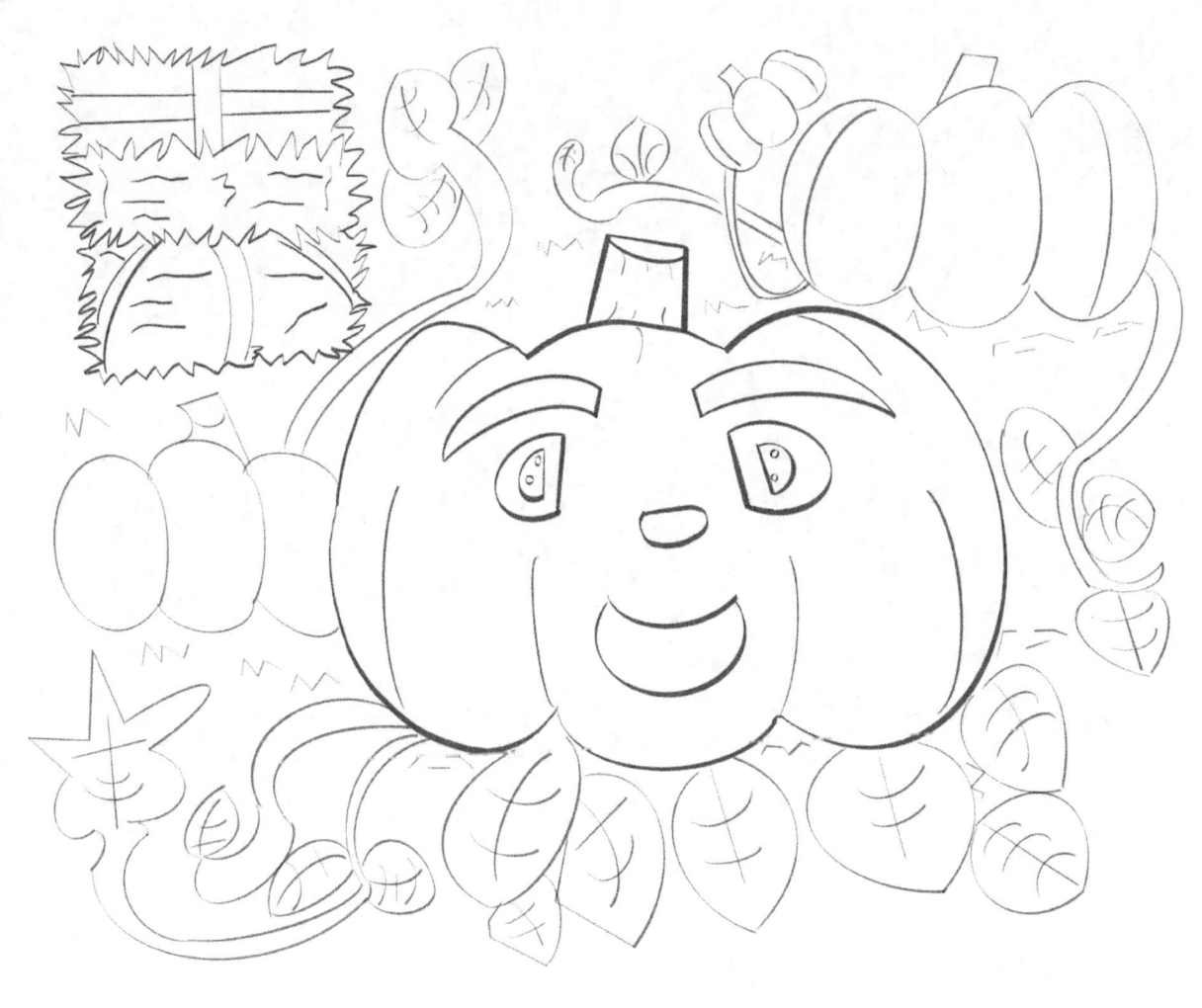

Halloween Fairy

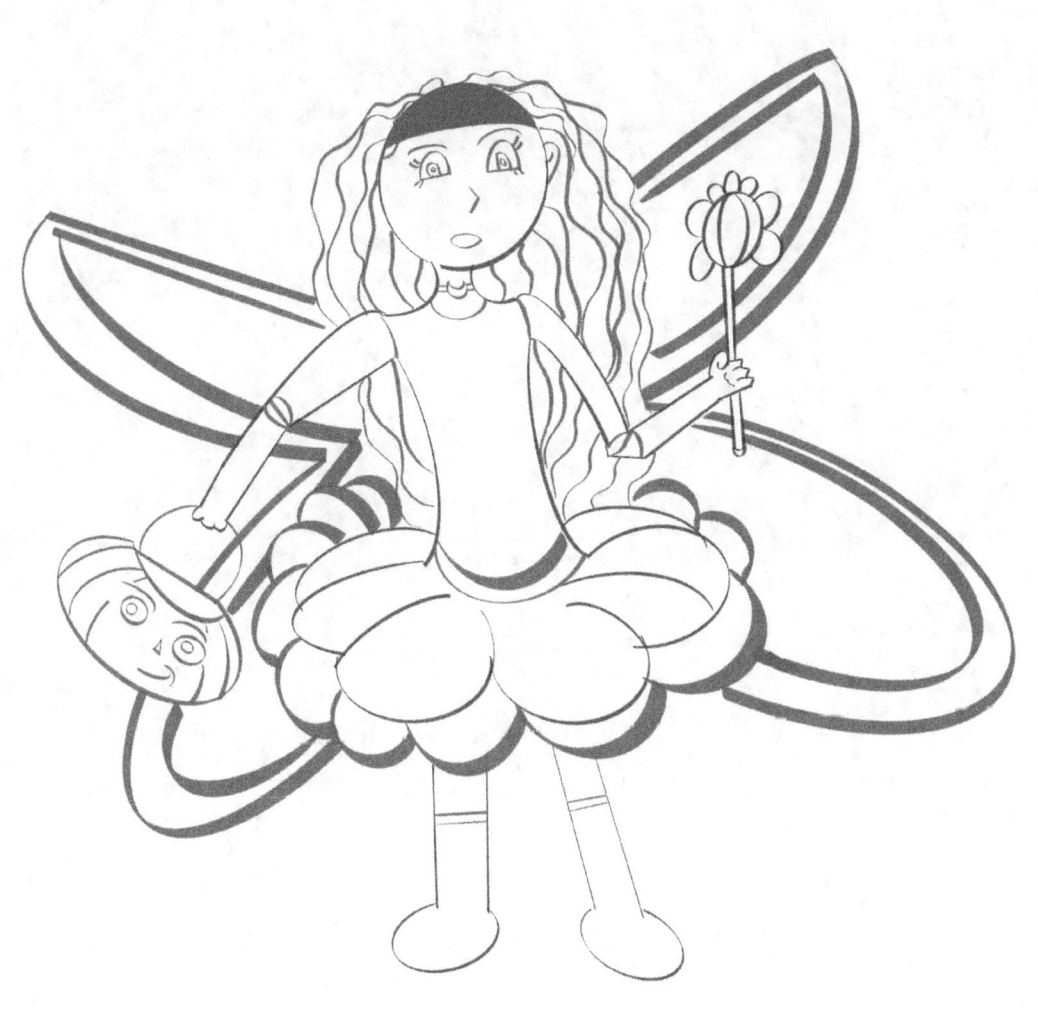

Kitten Girl

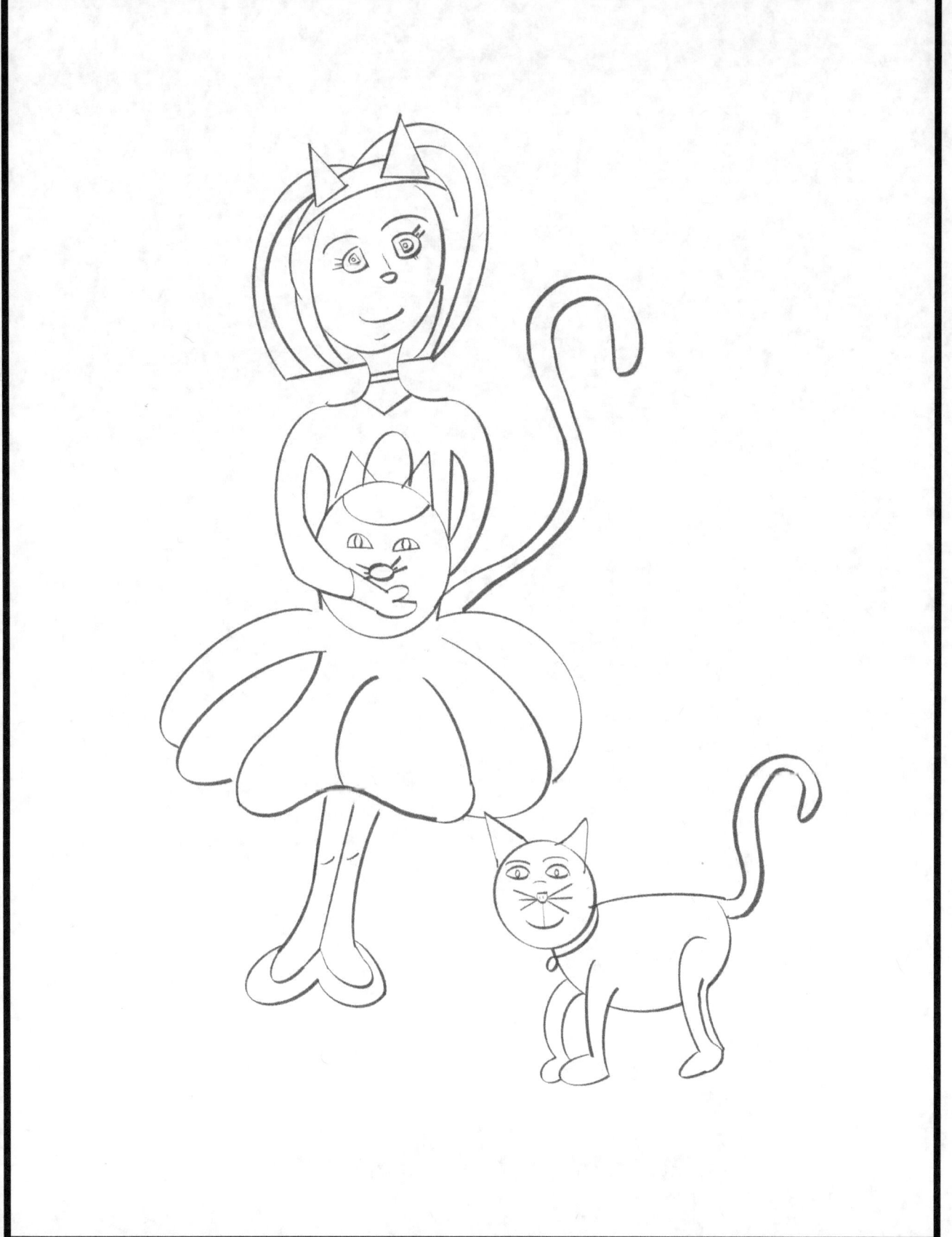

Frankenstein's Monster

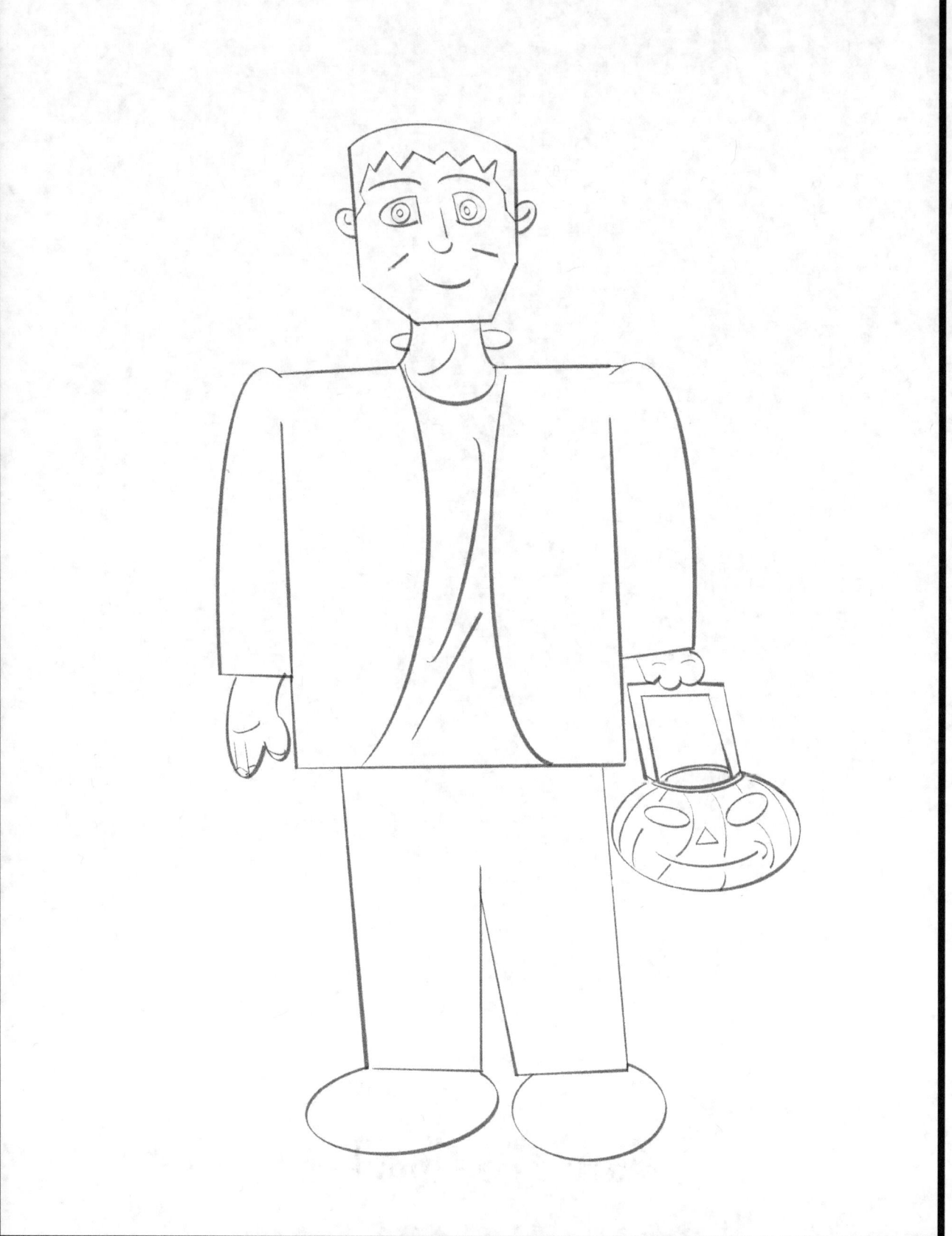

Gary the Ghoul

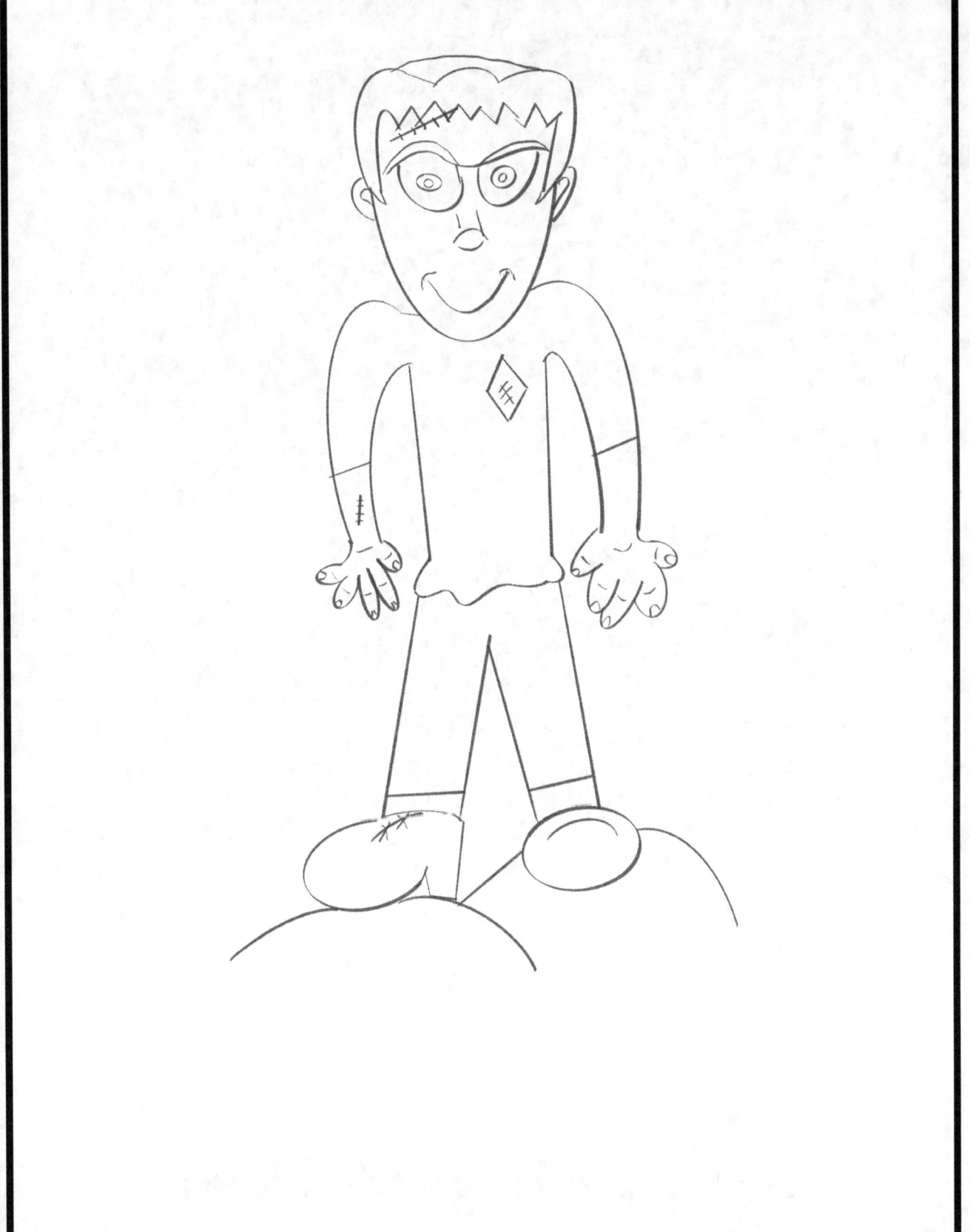

Ghost boy and his ghostly friends

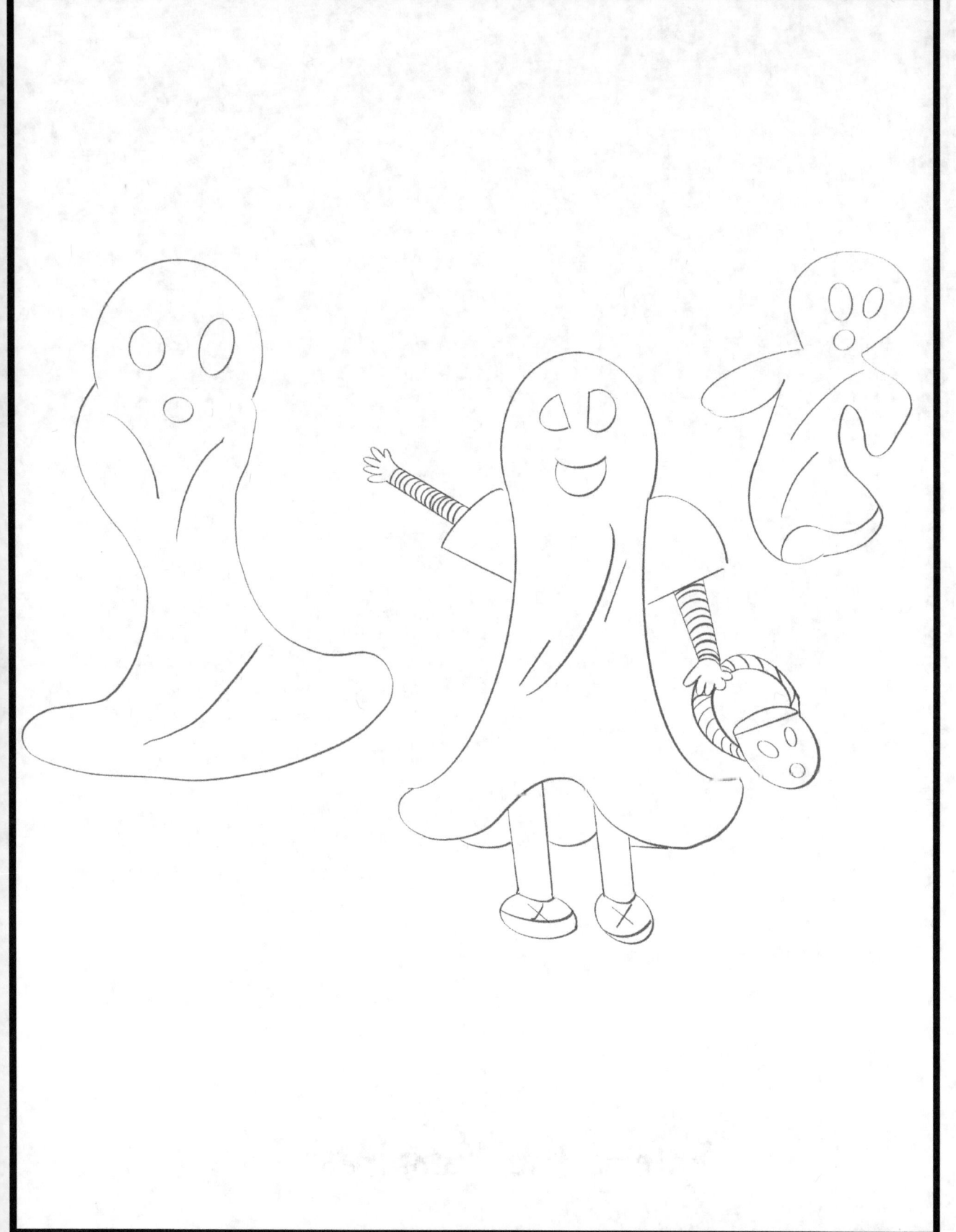

Valery the Vampiress

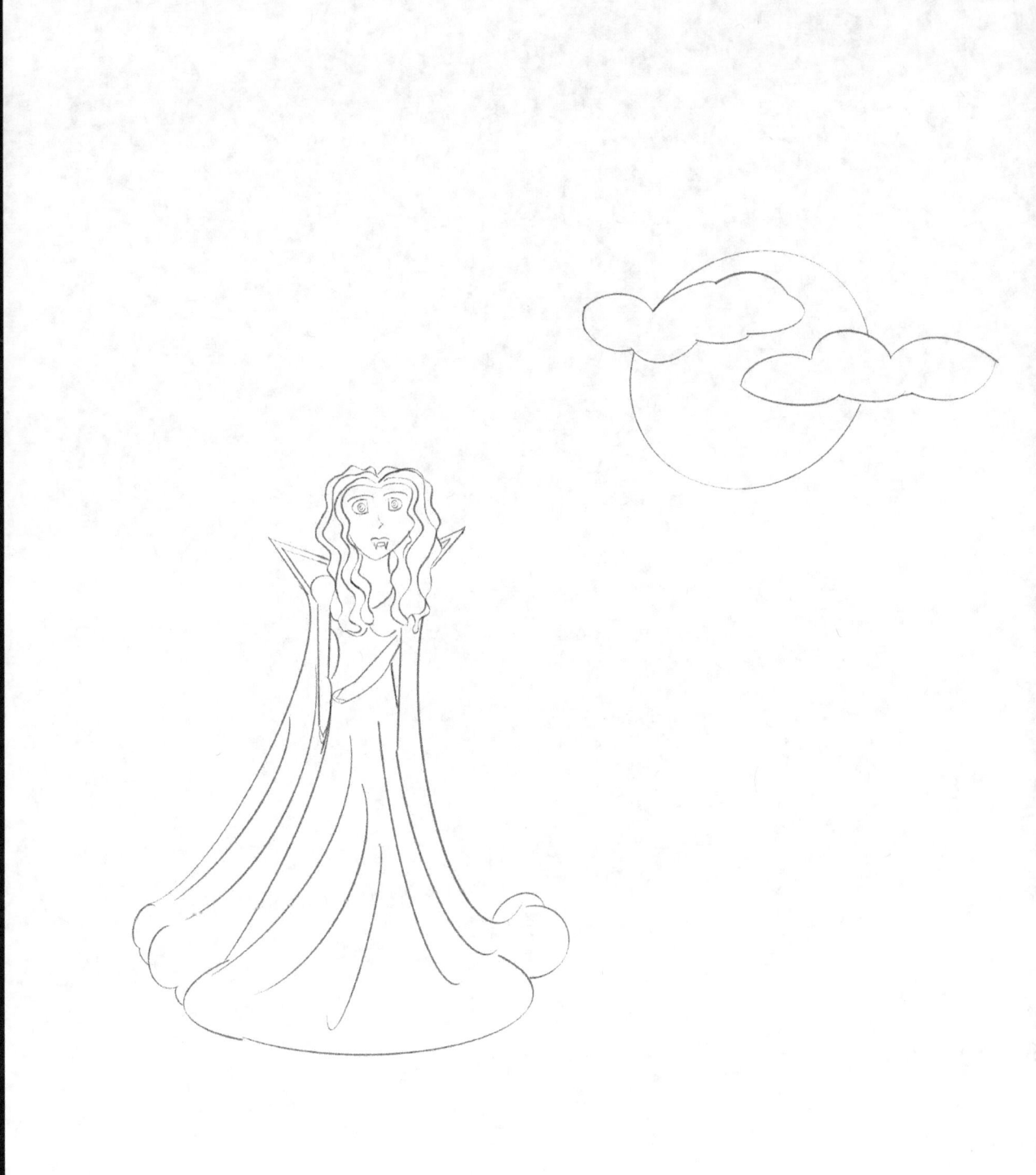

Dracula and Batrick

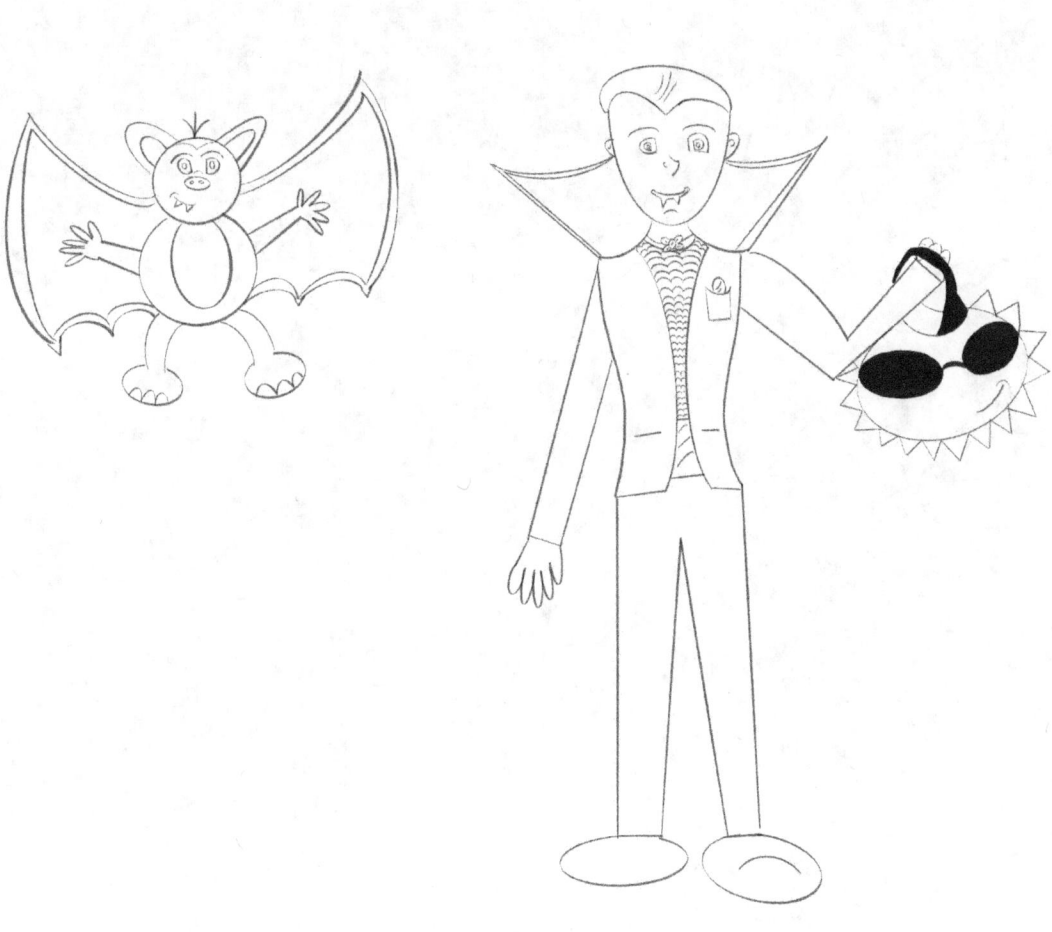

Manny the Mummy

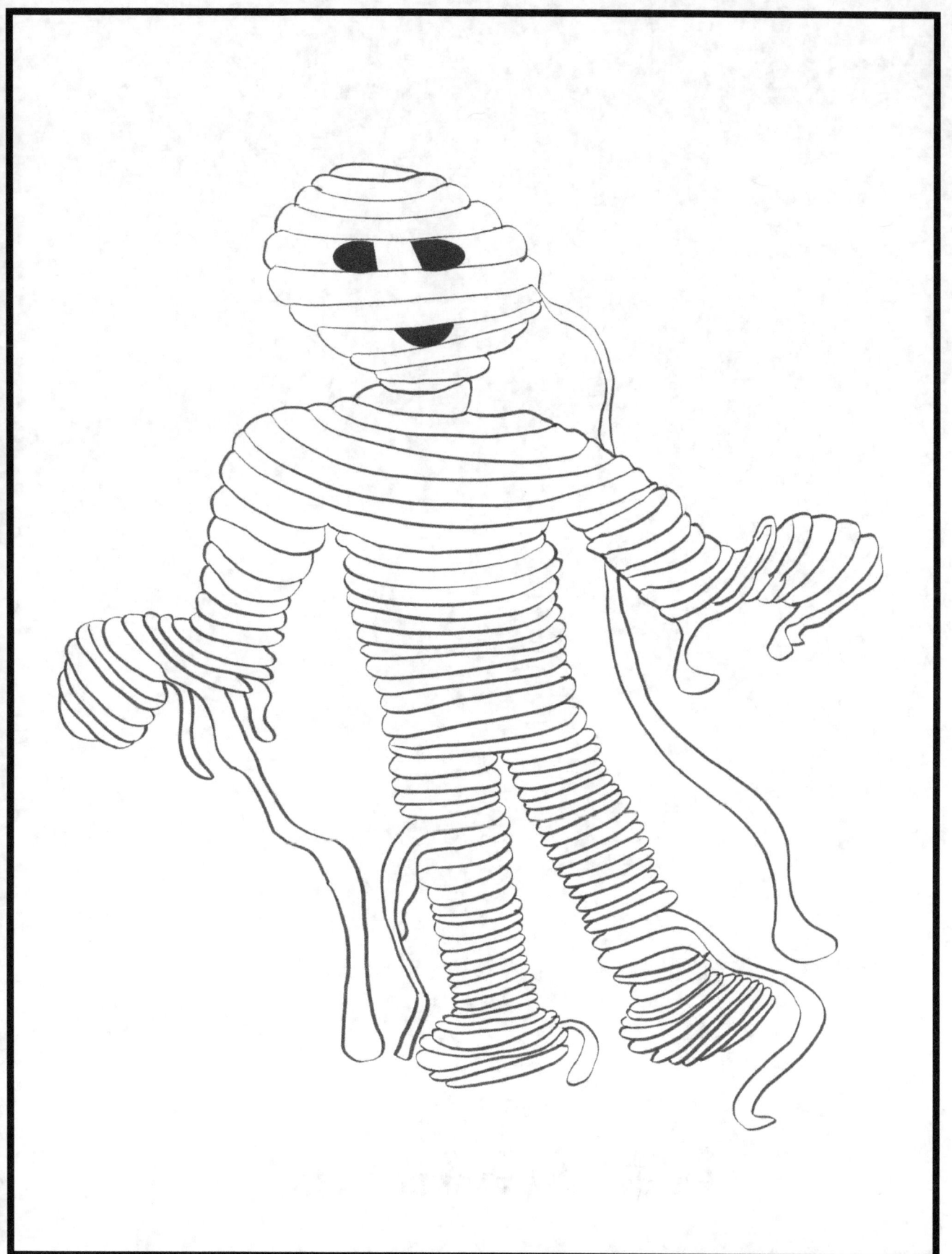

Bride of Frankenstein

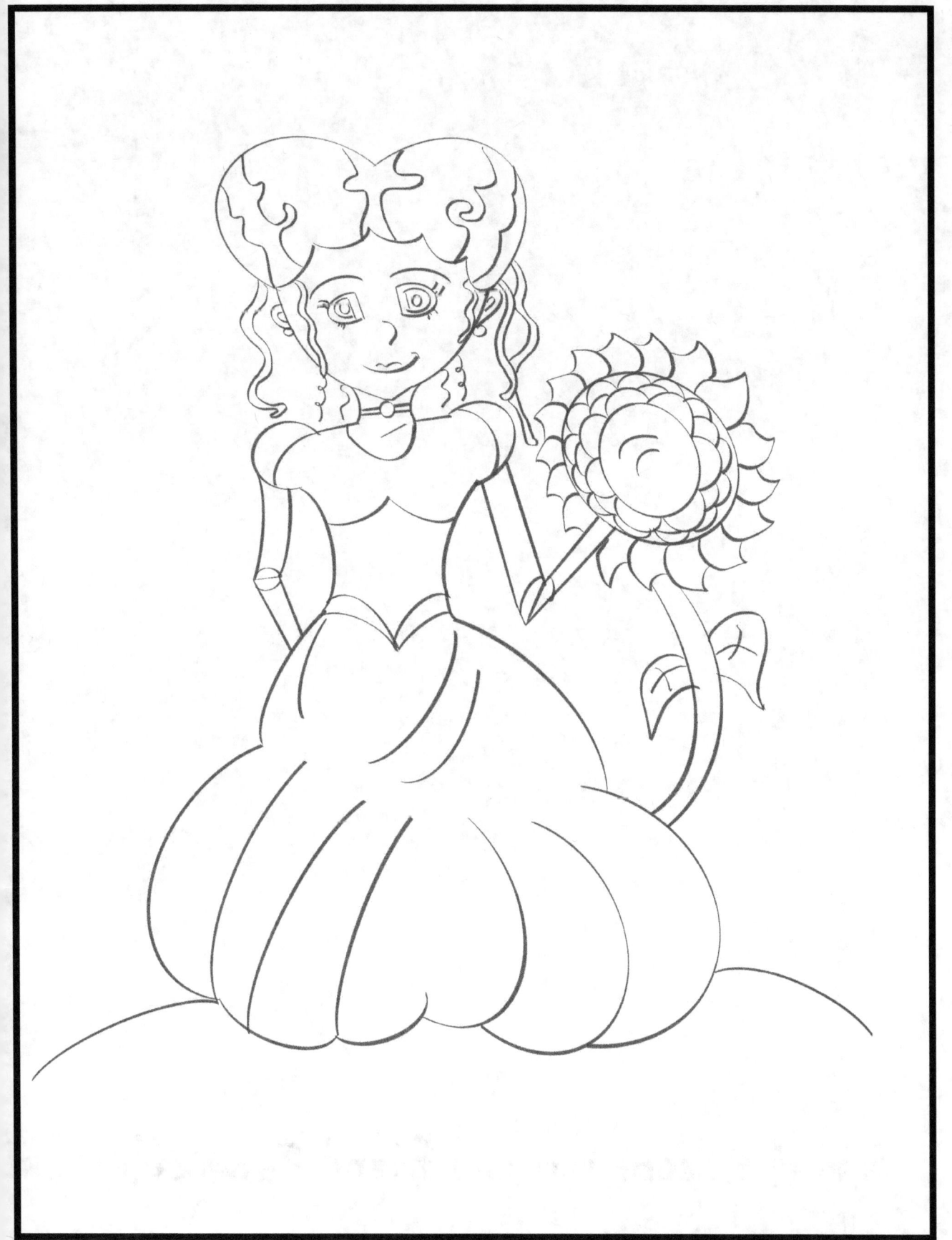

Sam the Scarecrow and friend Crowseph

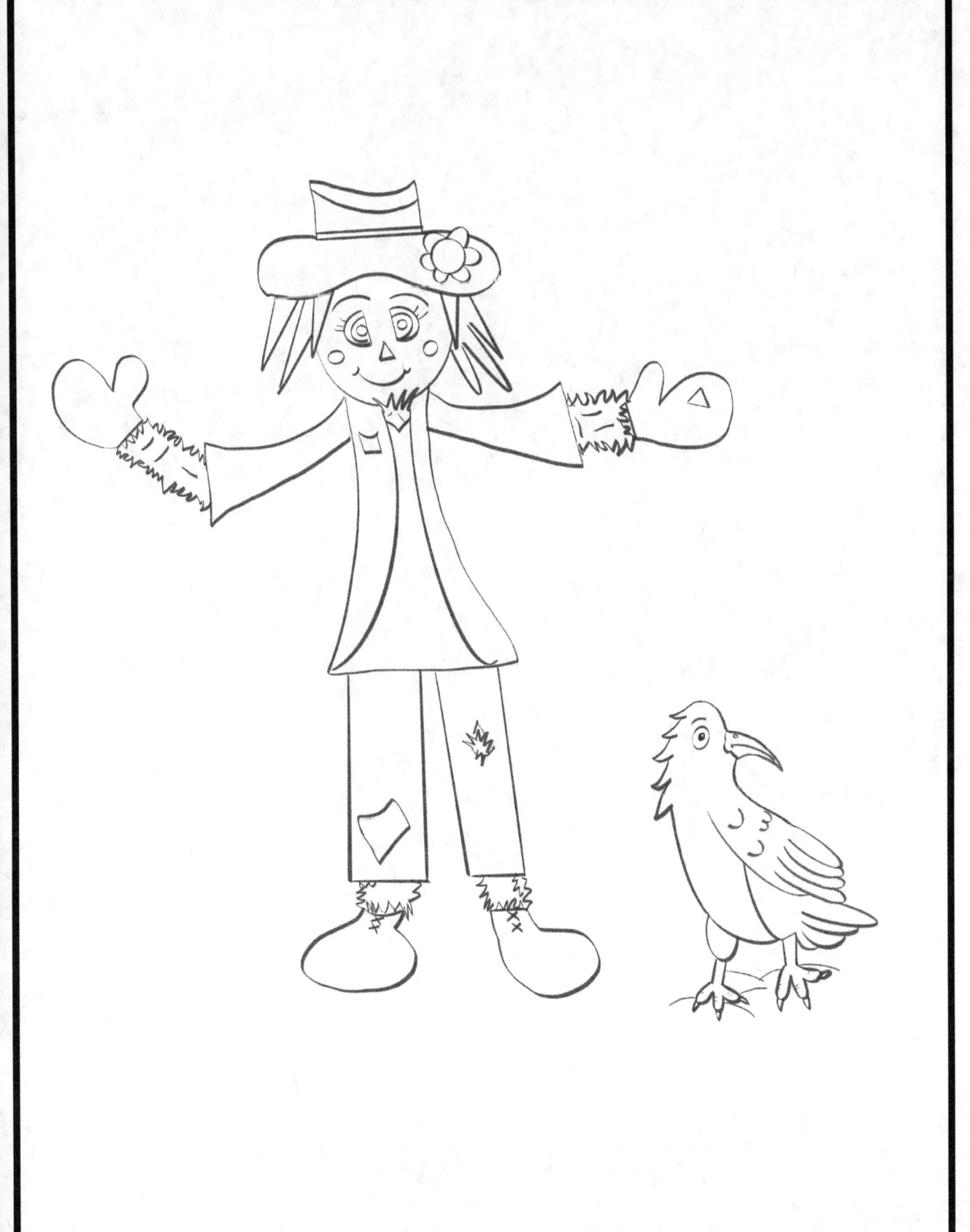

Stason the Werewolf

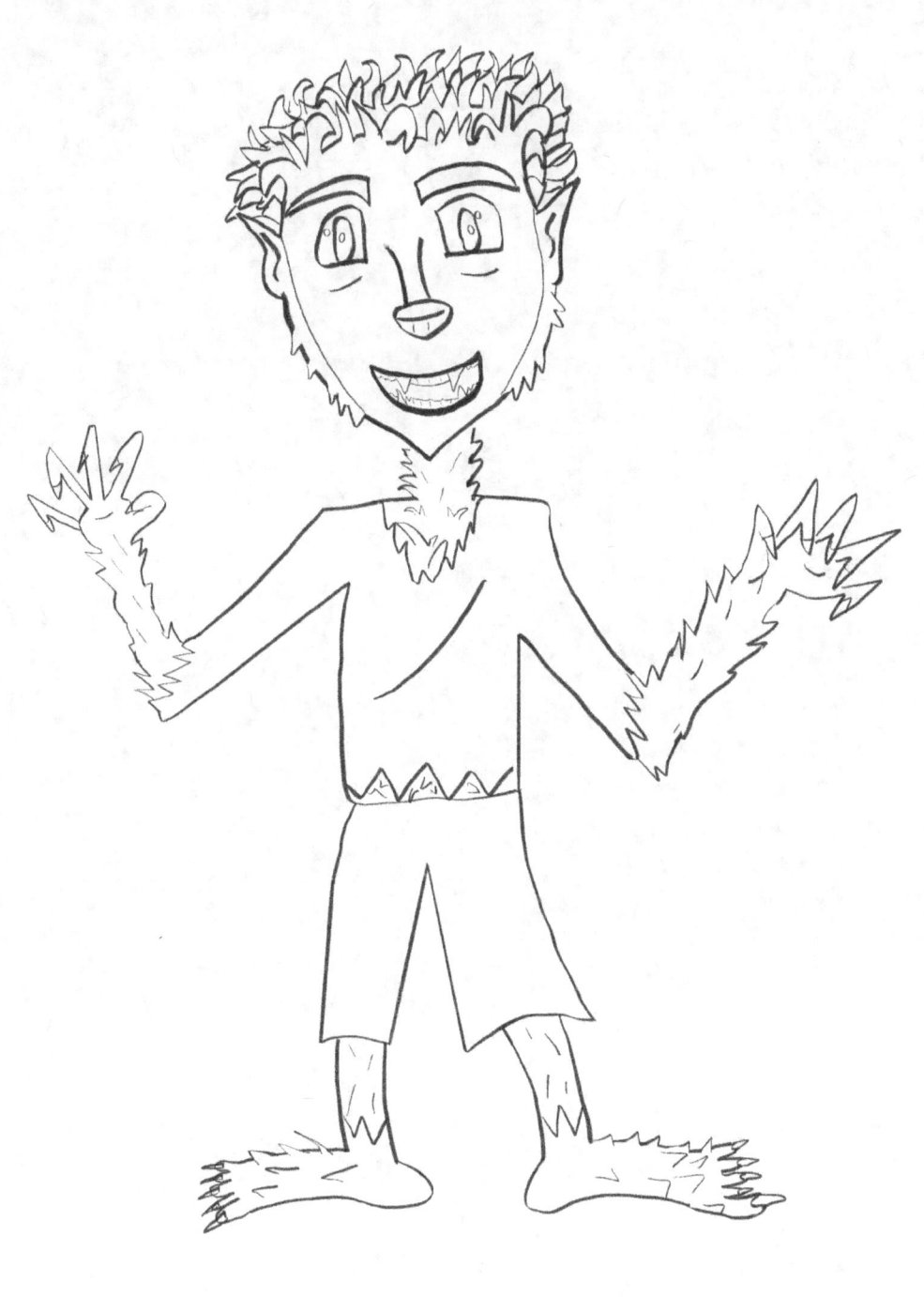

Tatum the Witch

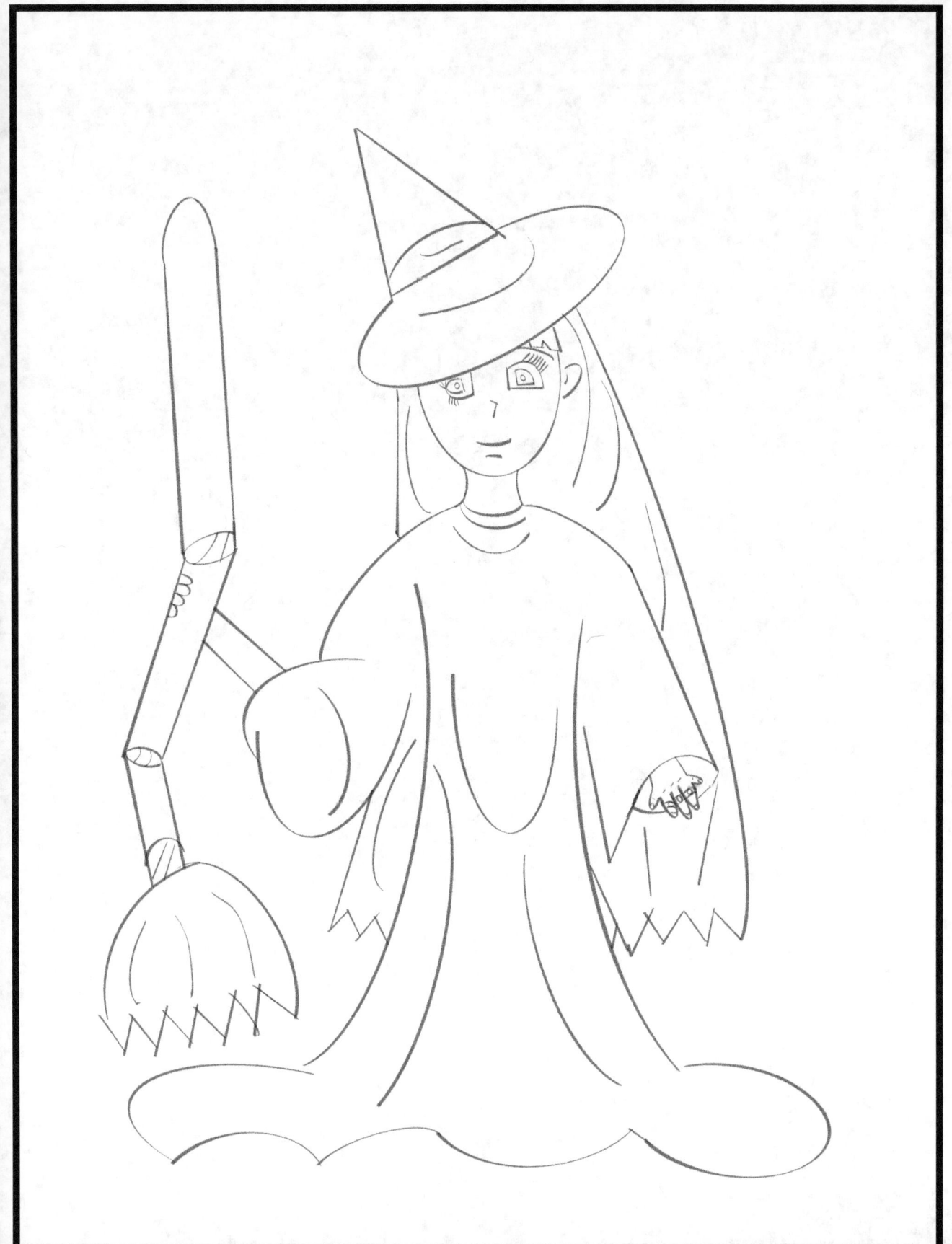